The Life of a
SALMON

Clare Hibbert

Raintree

Chicago, Illinois

© 2005 Raintree
Published by Raintree, a division of
Reed Elsevier, Inc.
Chicago, IL 60602
Customer Service 888-363-4266
Visit our website at www.raintreelibrary.com

For more information address the publisher:
Raintree, 100 N. LaSalle, Suite 1200
Chicago IL 60602

Printed and bound in China by the South China
Printing Company
08 07 06 05 04
10 9 8 7 6 5 4 3 2 1

Library of Congress Cataloging-in-Publication Data

Hibbert, Clare, 1970-
   Life of a salmon / Clare Hibbert.
      p. cm. -- (Life cycles)
   Includes bibliographical references (p.30).
   ISBN 1-4109-0543-8 (library binding) --
   1. Salmon--Life cycles--Juvenile literature. I. Title.
II. Series: Hibbert, Clare, 1970-   Life cycles.
   QL638.S2H53 2004
   597.5'6--dc22

                   2004002718

Acknowledgments
The publishers would like to thank the following
for permission to reproduce photographs:
p. 4 National Geographic/Getty Images; p. 5
David T. Grewcock/FLPA; p. 8 G. Bernard/NHPA;
p. 9 Corbis; p. 10 Stone/Getty Images; pp. 11, 12,
16 Natural Visions; p. 13, 15 P. Morris/Ardea; p. 14
John Robinson/Woodfall Wild Images; p. 17 Chris
Martin Bahr/Ardea; p. 18 Jason Hawkes Aerial
Photolibrary; p. 19 Getty Images; p. 20
Foto Natura/FLPA; p. 21 Gerard Lacz/FLPA; p.
22 Sue Scott/Woodfall Wild Images; p. 23 Kevin
Schafer/NHPA; p. 24 Francois Gohier/Ardea; p. 25
John Shaw/NHPA; p. 26 Trevor McDonald/NHPA;
p. 27 Jean-Louis Le Moigne/NHPA; p. 28 Dan
Griggs/NHPA; p. 29 Art Wolfe/Science Photo
Library.

Cover photograph of an Atlantic salmon,
reproduced with permission of Oxford Scientific
Films (Keith Ringland).

The publishers would like to thank Janet Stott
for her assistance in the preparation of this book.

Contents

Any words appearing in bold, **like this,** are explained
in the Glossary.

The Salmon

Salmon are a type of fish. Like all fish they live in water. They have smooth, scale-covered bodies with fins that allow them to swim. Like you they need to breathe in a gas called **oxygen,** which they take from the water using **gills.** Gills are special body parts found under slits on the side of their heads.

Salmon babies hatch from eggs that are laid in **freshwater** streams and rivers. As adults, they spend most of their lives in the ocean.

These adult salmon are swimming in the ocean.

eye   gill   fin

tail

Growing up

Just as you grow bigger year after year, the salmon grows and changes, too. The different stages of its life make up its **life cycle.** There are different types of salmon and they all go through the same life stages.

Where in the world?

Adult salmon live in the oceans. There are two main types of salmon. The Atlantic salmon lives in the Atlantic Ocean and the Pacific salmon lives in the Pacific Ocean.

When baby salmon first hatch, they don't look much like their parents.

A Salmon's Life

The **life cycle** of a salmon begins in the spring, when salmon eggs hatch in streams. The young fish live in rivers and **estuaries** for one to three years. The salmon then **migrates,** or travels, to its ocean feeding grounds. It spends up to eight years at sea, slowly gaining weight. Finally it is fully grown and ready to **spawn,** laying eggs that will develop into new salmon.

Making young

Both males and females leave the ocean to make the long, dangerous journey upstream to their **spawning grounds.** The female lays her eggs in a stream. Most salmon die a few days after spawning.

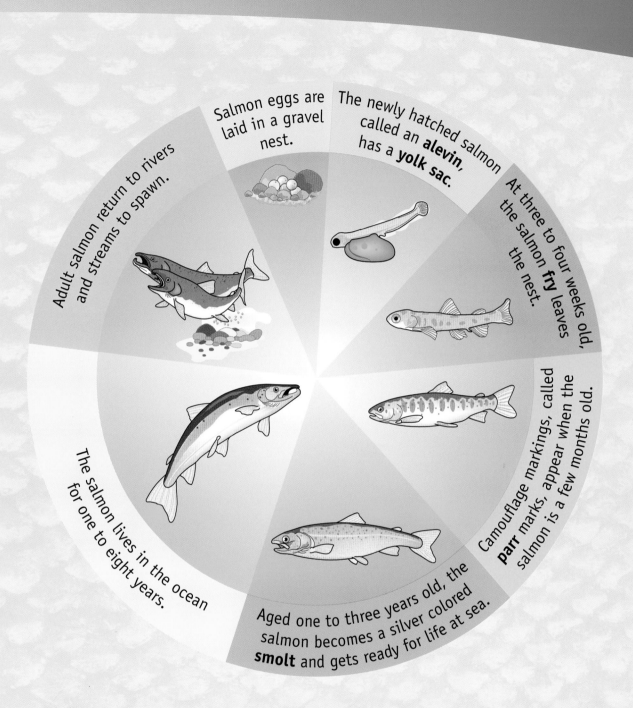

Salmon eggs are laid in a gravel nest.

The newly hatched salmon called an **alevin**, has a **yolk sac**.

At three to four weeks old, the salmon **fry** leaves the nest.

Camouflage markings, called **parr** marks, appear when the salmon is a few months old.

Aged one to three years old, the salmon becomes a silver colored **smolt** and gets ready for life at sea.

The salmon lives in the ocean for one to eight years.

Adult salmon return to rivers and streams to spawn.

This diagram shows the life cycle of a salmon, from egg to adult.

A Watery Nest

The female salmon lays her eggs in streams that have bubbling water. She buries the eggs in a shallow, gravel nest called a **redd.**

The eggs need cool, clean water. Shady trees along the bank keep the water from becoming too warm. The gravel nest lets water through, which washes around the eggs and keeps them clean.

Healthy salmon eggs are pinkish orange in color.

Survivors

Not all the eggs survive. Sometimes a redd is destroyed by people or animals crossing the stream. Sometimes the eggs die because conditions are not quite right. Eggs that have died turn a milky white color. Inside each healthy egg a baby salmon, or **embryo,** is developing. After two months it is ready to hatch.

Egg eaters

Although they are hidden under the gravel, some of the salmon eggs are sniffed out by hungry hunters. Crayfish and trout love to snack on salmon eggs.

Crayfish live in freshwater lakes, rivers, and streams. They eat salmon eggs, fish, insects, and plants.

Hatching

It is early spring. The salmon eggs are about to hatch. Newly hatched salmon are called **alevins.** Each is about 1 inch (2–3 centimeters) long and has a balloon-like bag hanging from its body. This is its **yolk sac.** It contains enough food for the alevin to survive for about a month.

A yolk sac attached to the alevin's body is its own food supply.

Home, sweet home

The alevin stays in the safety of the **redd.** Its body needs to become stronger and grow fins so that it will be able to swim. For now the alevin can only move short distances by swishing its tail from side to side.

Teething

While the alevin is soaking up the yolk sac, its body is getting ready for life outside the nest. Inside the alevin's mouth, sharp teeth begin to push through the gums.

As the alevins grow, their yolk sacs get smaller. That is because the young fish are slowly using up the food.

Small Fry

After three to six weeks, the **alevin** has used up its **yolk sac.** Now it is called a **fry.** It must swim out of the **redd** and hunt for its own food. At first it feeds on **microscopic** animals and plants. As it grows bigger, it eats insects that live in the water. The fry grows scales all over its body. Scales are like a suit of armor that protects the fish.

The salmon fry swims out into the stream.

Beginning a journey

The fry starts to head downstream. It swims in a school, or large group, with hundreds of other fry. Some of them are eaten by larger fish, such as pike, sturgeon, or even other salmon.

Sink or swim

Inside the fry's body is a sausage shaped balloon. This is its swim bladder, and it fills with air the first time the fry swims. The swim bladder allows the fish to keep at a certain level in the water, without sinking to the bottom or floating to the surface. The salmon can squeeze or relax it in order to float or sink in the water.

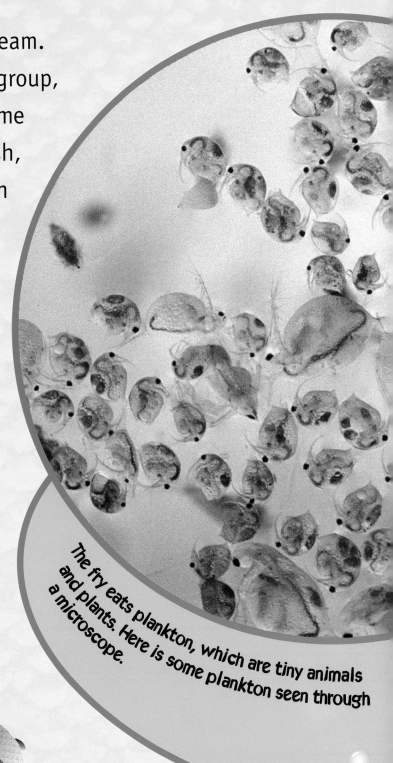

The fry eats plankton, which are tiny animals and plants. Here is some plankton seen through a microscope.

Spots and Marks

As the **fry** grows, spots and stripes appear on its body. These are called **parr** marks, and the fish is now known as a parr. The markings help to **camouflage,** or hide, the fish among the weeds. They make it harder for **predators** to spot the fish. Herons and other water birds like to feed on parrs.

Parrs develop marks on their skin that help them hide from predators.

Growing and eating

By now, the salmon is about 3 inches (7 centimeters) long. As well as insects, its diet includes shrimp, tadpoles, and fish eggs. The parr has an amazing appetite! It stays in the river for months or even years, growing bigger and stronger.

Slime

The salmon's body is covered with a thin layer of slime, called mucus. This helps to protect its scales if the fish rubs against sharp stones on the river bed. The mucus also makes the fish slippery and harder for a predator to catch!

The parrs dart around the stream, hunting for food.

Silvery Smolt

When it is one to three years old, the salmon loses its brown **parr** marks. At this stage of its life, the salmon is called a **smolt.** Now it has silvery sides, a bluish green back, and a pale belly. Its new coloring gives it excellent **camouflage** in the open ocean.

The smolt looks a little like an adult salmon, only much smaller.

Water worlds

The smolt is about 6 inches (15 centimeters) long, but it is not quite ready for life at sea. Until now it has been used to living in freshwater. Its body is going to have to make some big changes before it will be able to cope with the salty ocean water.

From its lookout a cormorant watches for movements in the water. It catches all sorts of fish to eat, including young salmon.

Attack from the air

Birds such as terns, gulls, and cormorants head inland to swoop down and catch smolts that are swimming toward the sea. These awesome seabirds gobble millions of the young fish. An adult cormorant may eat more than one hundred smolts in a single feeding session!

Adapting to Salt

The place where a river meets the sea is called an **estuary.** Estuary water is **brackish,** meaning it is a mix of freshwater from the river and salt water from the ocean.

This photograph of a river mouth, or estuary, was taken from the air. Salty seawater mixes with the river water when the tide comes in.

Getting ready

The **smolt** stays in the estuary for a few weeks or even months, getting used to the saltier water. The fish has a kidney inside its body that deals with waste. The kidney **adapts** to manage the extra salt. There are changes in the smolt's **gills,** too. The smolt needs to adapt slowly, but not all smolts get the chance. If the river floods, they might be washed out to sea before their bodies are ready. If this happens, the smolts die.

Waders

The smolt sticks to shallow marshes around the edge of the estuary, where it is less likely to be washed out to sea. There are dangers here, too. Wading birds such as herons search the marshes, hoping to spear fish with |their sharp beaks.

This fish has ended up in a kingfisher's beak.

Life at Sea

Now the salmon leaves the **estuary** and begins its life in the ocean. It will stay there for the next one to eight years, until it is fully grown.

Hunter and hunted

There is more food in the ocean than there was in the estuary, so the salmon grows very quickly. It relies on its senses of smell and sight to find food, such as small fish, shrimp, and squid.

Out in the ocean, salmon hunt together in schools.

At the same time, the salmon must avoid becoming someone else's meal. Fishing boats drop their nets to catch salmon, and there are animal **predators,** too. These include seals, sea lions, and killer whales.

Marine mammals

Although they live in the sea, killer whales, sea lions, and seals are closer relatives to you than to fish! Like you, they are **mammals.** They dive deep to hunt, but they need to come up to the surface every twenty minutes or so to breathe air.

The harbor seal is a swift hunter. Its diet includes salmon and other fish.

All Grown Up

Most salmon spend three or four years in the ocean, although some stay for up to eight years. During this time salmon swim thousands of miles searching for good feeding grounds. Some salmon grow as long as 5 feet (1.5 meters), though others reach only about 20 inches (50 centimeters).

Fully grown salmon are powerful swimmers.

Back to the river mouth

Once a salmon is fully grown, it is ready to have babies. It finds its way back to the **estuary** where it first entered the sea. The salmon stays in the estuary while its body **adapts** to the **brackish** water, which has less salt than the seawater. When its body has adjusted to freshwater, the salmon heads upriver.

Finding the way

No one knows exactly how the salmon finds its way back to its home stream. It may be that the fish recognizes different rivers and estuaries by their scent and just smells its way home!

Salmon that are ready to mate make their way back to the estuary.

Heading Home

Traveling upstream is hard work. The salmon's body is large and strong, though. It is powerful enough to swim against the **current.** Even a small waterfall is not a problem. The salmon flings itself out of the water and onto the higher level. The salmon does not stop to feed. It lives off stored fats in its body. All of its efforts go into the journey.

Salmon can throw themselves up and over a small waterfall.

Bold and bright

As it swims, the salmon changes color. The male's coloring is different than the female's. He may be green, brown, pink, or red. This will help him to attract a female at the **spawning ground.**

Danger!

Predators have been waiting for the **salmon run.** Wild cats, wolves, bears, and eagles visit the river. Humans fishing is also a danger to the salmon.

Grizzly bears wait with jaws open, ready to grab the leaping salmon.

Nests of Eggs

At the **spawning ground,** the male and female salmon pair up. The female uses her tail to dig a shallow **redd** in the gravel. Then she pushes her back fin down into the redd and begins to lay her eggs. The male swims alongside and spreads his **sperm,** which is called milt, over the eggs to **fertilize** them.

The female waits for a male to swim up. He will fertilize her eggs as she drops them into the redd.

Thousands of eggs!

Using her tail the female covers the redd and then starts to dig another. The salmon pair continue to dig and **spawn** until the female has used up all her eggs. Depending on her size, she can lay between 2,500 and 7,000 eggs.

A fish ladder like this one allows spawning salmon to make their way past a dam.

Finding a way

Dams are useful for people, but they block the way to spawning grounds and stop salmon from finding the right conditions to lay eggs. At some dams, though, people have built fish ladders. These are pools with steps that allow the salmon to swim up the side of the dam.

Worn Out

After they have **spawned,** the male and female salmon are weak and worn out. The long journey upstream has used up all their energy. They guard the **redd** for a few days, but soon die of tiredness. The dead fish are a meal for many animals. This includes even the new **fry** when they head downstream in a few months!

Dying or dead salmon make an easy meal for animals such as this mink.

Starting again

A few types of salmon do not always die after spawning. They rest for a while and then head back downstream. When they reach the **estuary,** they wait while their bodies get used to the salt again. Then they return to the ocean, where there is plenty to eat.

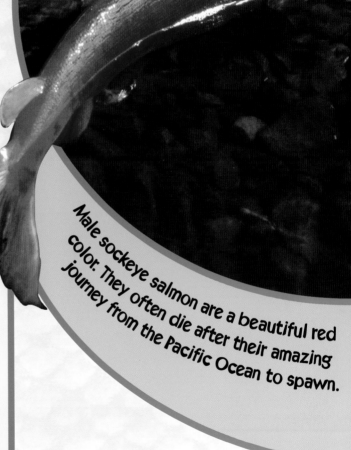

Male sockeye salmon are a beautiful red color. They often die after their amazing journey from the Pacific Ocean to spawn.

Salmon farms

Not all salmon live their whole lives in the wild. At salmon hatcheries eggs and milt are collected from adult salmon that have been caught. The baby salmon are raised at the hatchery, out of reach of **predators,** then released into the wild. Salmon farms are different. Here adult salmon are raised for food in ocean cages.

Find Out for Yourself

The best way to find out more about the life cycle of a fish is to keep your own. You cannot keep pet salmon but you can keep goldfish. You can also find out more by reading books about salmon and other fish, and by looking for information on the Internet.

Books to read

Baxter, John. *Worldlife Library: Salmon*. Stillwater, Minn.: Voyageur Press, 2002.

Spilsbury, Louise, and Richard Spilsbury. *From Egg to Adult: The Life Cycle of a Fish*. Chicago: Heinemann Library, 2003.

Using the Internet

Explore the Internet to find out more about salmon. Websites can change, so if some of the links below no longer work, don't worry. Use a search engine, such as www.yahooligans.com, and type in keywords such as "salmon," "smolt," and "life cycle."

Websites

www.enchantedlearning.com/subjects/fish/printouts/Salmon.shtml
Learn more about salmon and print out pictures to color in and keep.
www.jsd.k12.ak.us/ab/jones_cl/jones.htm
Take a look at this class project from a school in Alaska. It is all about the life cycle of salmon.

Glossary

adapt to slowly change to deal with new conditions

alevin newly hatched salmon that is still living in its redd

brackish a mix of freshwater and saltwater

camouflage coloring or marks on an animal that match its surroundings, making it hard for predators to spot

current flow of water moving in one direction

dam place where a river has been blocked

embryo baby animal before it has hatched from an egg or been born

estuary lowest part of a river where it meets the ocean

fertilize to join together male and female parts to create the beginnings of a new living thing

fry young river salmon that has absorbed its yolk sac, but not yet developed parr marks

gill special body part that allows fish to take oxygen out of the water to breathe

life cycle all the different stages in the life of a living thing

mammal animal that gives birth to live young and feeds them milk

microscopic describes something so small that it can be seen only with the help of a microscope

migrate journey from one habitat or place to another at a particular time of year

oxygen gas in the air that living things need to breathe to stay alive

parr young river salmon that is between the fry and smolt stages and has camouflage markings

predator animal that hunts other animals for food

redd gravel nest where a salmon lays its eggs

salmon run journey of salmon to their spawning grounds

smolt young river salmon that has silvery sides and a blueish green back

spawn to reproduce. The female lays her eggs and the male covers them with milt to fertilize them.

spawning ground place where a salmon goes to spawn

sperm male sex cells

yolk sac food attached to the body of a newly hatched salmon, or alevin

Index

DATE DUE

DEC 0 0 2005	WITHDRAWN
SEP 1 2 2006	
JUN 2 8 2007	
SEP 1 1 2008	
OCT 7 2008	
AUG 1 9 2009	
DEC 1 2010	WITHDRAWN
WITHDRAWN	